SACRED SOLOS

Compiled
Arranged and Edited
by CLAIR W. JOHNSON

for E♭ Alto Saxophone with Piano Accompaniment

CONTENTS

VOLUMES IN THIS SERIES

C Flute and Piano

B♭ Clarinet and Piano

B♭ Cornet or Trumpet (Baritone 𝄞) and Piano

● E♭ Alto Saxophone and Piano

Trombone or Baritone 𝄢 and Piano

Each volume varies in contents and arrangements to favor the instrument concerned.

RUBANK®

HAL•LEONARD®
CORPORATION

7777 W. BLUEMOUND RD. P.O. BOX 13819 MILWAUKEE, WI 53213

Where'er You Walk

from Semele

G. F. HANDEL
Arr. by Clair W. Johnson

Agnus Dei

GEORGES BIZET
Arr. by Clair W. Johnson

6

Ave Maria

FR. SCHUBERT
Arr. by Clair W. Johnson

10

Ave Maria 4 (Schubert)

Ave Maria 4 (Schubert)

If With All Your Hearts

from Elijah

FELIX MENDELSSOHN
Arr. by Clair W. Johnson

If With All Your Hearts 3

The Rosary

ETHELBERT NEVIN
Arr. by Clair W. Johnson

Calvary

PAUL RODNEY
Arr. by Clair W. Johnson

(47) Giubiloso

(65) Andante

p con espress.

The Holy City

STEPHEN ADAMS
Arr. by Clair W. Johnson

Andante moderato

Solo Part

SACRED SOLOS

Compiled
Arranged and Edited
by CLAIR W. JOHNSON

for Eb Alto Saxophone with Piano Accompaniment

CONTENTS

VOLUMES IN THIS SERIES

C Flute and Piano   Bb Clarinet and Piano

Bb Cornet or Trumpet (Baritone 𝄞) and Piano

● Eb Alto Saxophone and Piano   Trombone or Baritone 𝄢 and Piano

Each volume varies in contents and arrangements to favor the instrument concerned.

RUBANK®

HAL•LEONARD®
CORPORATION

7777 W. BLUEMOUND RD. P.O. BOX 13819 MILWAUKEE, WI 53213

Where'er You Walk
from Semele

G. F. HANDEL
Arr. by Clair W. Johnson

E♭ Alto Saxophone

Agnus Dei

Eb Alto Saxophone

GEORGES BIZET
Arr. by Clair W. Johnson

Ave Maria

Eb Alto Saxophone

FR. SCHUBERT
Arr. by Clair W. Johnson

If With All Your Hearts

from Elijah

Eb Alto Saxophone

FELIX MENDELSSOHN
Arr. by Clair W. Johnson

The Rosary

Eb Alto Saxophone

ETHELBERT NEVIN
Arr. by Clair W. Johnson

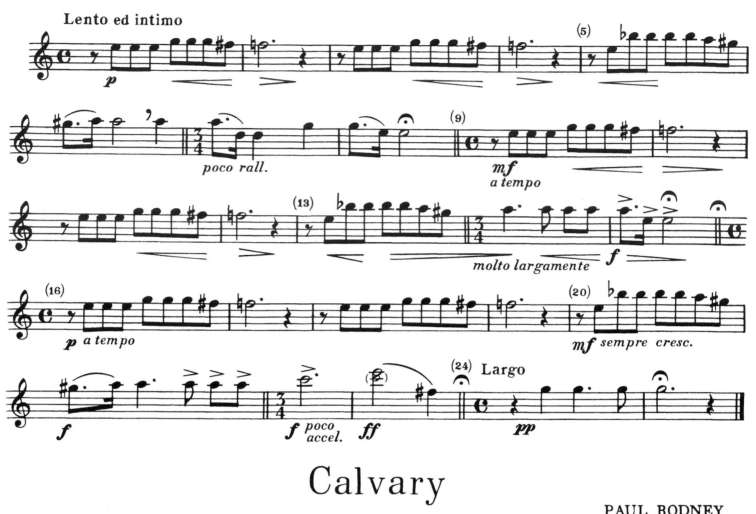

Calvary

PAUL RODNEY
Arr. by Clair W. Johnson

8

The Holy City

Eb Alto Saxophone

STEPHEN ADAMS
Arr. by Clair W. Johnson

Panis Angelicus

CÉSAR FRANCK
Arr. by Clair W. Johnson

Adoration

E♭ Alto Saxophone

FELIX BOROWSKI
Arr. by Clair W. Johnson

Meditation

Eb Alto Saxophone

JULES MASSENET
Arr. by Clair W. Johnson

Ave Maria

BACH-GOUNOD
Arr. by Clair W. Johnson

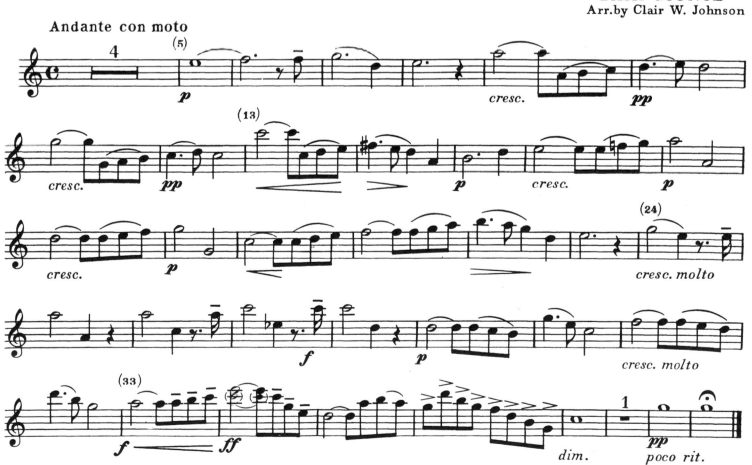

Alleluja
from Exsultate Jubilate

Eb Alto Saxophone

W. A. MOZART
Arr. by Clair W. Johnson

Panis Angelicus

CÉSAR FRANCK
Arr. by Clair W. Johnson

Adoration

FELIX BOROWSKI
Arr. by Clair W. Johnson

Eb Alto Saxophone

Piano

(39) **Allegro agitato**

Meditation

JULES MASSENET
Arr. by Clair W. Johnson

Meditation 4

Meditation 4

Ave Maria

BACH-GOUNOD
Arr. by Clair W. Johnson

Ave Maria 3 (Bach-Gounod)

42

Ave Maria 3 (Bach-Gounod)

Alleluja
from Exsultate Jubilate

W. A. MOZART
Arr. by Clair W. Johnson

44

46

Alleluja 6

Alleluja 6

(135)

(143)

cresc.

cresc.

Alleluja 6